A Handbook for the Middle School Parent

NINE WAYS TO HELP YOUR CHILD SUCCEED

Victoria Cummings M.Ed

Website: www.thrivingstudent.com
Email: victoria@thrivingstudent.com

ISBN: 1453870679
ISBN-13: 9781453870679
Library of Congress Control Number: 2010915055

The Middle School Parent Handbook comes of Victoria's 20 plus years of experience in education. She really "gets" the middle school child. Throughout the handbook Victoria's passion, commitment, and caring come through as if she were having a personal conversation with you.

This is a practical manual that not only educates, but also gives hands-on tips and strategies you can use immediately.

If you have or are about to have a middle school student, this is a must have handbook.

Jeffrey A. Betman, Ph.D.
Child Psychologist and Author

Special Acknowledgements

The publishing of this book was made possible by a grant from the Hazel Montague Hutcheson Foundation in agreement with Inner city Ministry.

A special thank you to all of the middle school children I have ever taught. It was a joy to teach you and watch you grow into young adults. Thank you for allowing me to be a part of your lives, and for being part of mine.

Contents

PREFACE

This handbook comes after a twenty-three year career in education. During this tenure, I had the joy and privilege of teaching both elementary and middle school students. Over the years, many have asked which grade level I preferred. I could not answer that question anymore than a parent could choose a favorite child. Each grade level is unique, endearing, and rewarding in its own way. My response to this question was always simple; I enjoyed them all.

During my years in the school system, I got to know many parents. We worked together in various ways, from conferences and committees to school socials and volunteer work. It was in the middle grades that I noticed a deeper level of parent concern and frustration.

In the eyes of many parents, their amiable elementary children had gone and less agreeable middle school students had taken their place. Parents struggled with ways to understand their children. Many simply did not know what to do next. A small percentage of parents simply gave up. But, most parents walked the extra mile to get their children through this period of change.

The School Is There To Help

This handbook serves as a reminder to parents that resources are available through the school system. Parents should feel comfortable about using these resources. If your child has an issue, school professionals can work with you to find solutions.

> Remember,
> You, the teachers, counselors and administrators–are working toward the same goal:
>
> **To do what is best for your child.**

This Handbook is One of Many Parent Resources

This handbook is based on years of personal experience, observations, and research. It was created in an effort to help parents better understand their adolescent children. In no way does it cover all that could be said on the vast topic of middle school students; an entire set of encyclopedias would not be sufficient. There are many books on adolescence. Look through materials at public libraries or bookstores to find topics of interest to you. The more you know about this phase of your children's lives, the better equipped you will be to keep them safe and growing in a positive direction.

This text is not intended to serve where a counselor or professional help is needed. If your child needs help, please seek the advice of a professional. Your school system can offer guidance in this area.

Getting a child through the adolescent years tends to be a challenge for many. It takes time and effort on the part of the parent to keep their child safe and happy and moving in a positive direction. As complicated as it seems sometimes, remember that good parenting, love, and support are all a child ever needs. In all my years as an educator, I have never met a parent who did not think his or her child was worth the effort.

"*The hardest part of raising a child is teaching them to ride bicycles. A shaky child on a bicycle for the first time needs both support and freedom. The realization that this is what the child will always need can hit hard.*"

~Sloan Wilson

Help Your Children Succeed
By Being Familiar with

1

ADOLESCENT CHARACTERISTICS

Middle school is a time when much emotional and social learning develop. Most students enjoy interacting with a variety of classmates, both academically and socially. This is a time when students explore and discover their interests. They join clubs and attend school sports or social events. In these years students learn about themselves and how they relate to others.

Common Middle School Student Traits
- Adolescents enjoy social interactions with classmates and most are eager to make new friends.
- School cliques begin to develop, and personal identity issues arise. Students often move from one peer group to the next as they explore the natural questions, "Who am I? How do I fit in?"
- Peer relationships become more important and peer opinion becomes more influential.
- Adolescents seek independence from family. Occasionally they are rude, disrespectful, or dismissive of parents in an attempt to break away

- Romantic feelings begin to develop and many students move in and out of relationships as they learn about themselves in this new way.
- Moody, unpredictable, or sullen behaviors are common.

Adolescents develop at their own unique time. Yet, some basic characteristics appear more often within each age group. Know that any of the behaviors described are middle school specific, yet all children are unique and your children may or may not experience any or all of these behaviors. Teachers are familiar with the characteristics of this age group and work with students in ways that complement their development.

Common Sixth Grade Characteristics

Most sixth graders start middle school feeling excited yet scared. Common worries are: will they be able to find their classes, will they be able remember their locker combination, will they know other classmates, and will older kids pick on them? In most schools, each grade level is located in separate sections of the building. This arrangement serves sixth graders particularly well. It helps to relieve anxiety and offers them a chance to get comfortable in their new surroundings.

Sixth grade is a year of much independence, which aid in preparing your child for the grades that follow. Students are expected to get necessary materials from home to locker to class each day without reminders. This presents a problem for many, as it is likely the first time they have needed to be self-reliant. Teachers are aware of this and help children adjust to the new responsibilities. Over time, patterns take shape making it easier for students to be more self-directed.

By October their fears have subsided. Most have settled into a routine and are at home in their new setting. They have made new friends, discovered extracurricular activities, and now enjoy a growing sense of independence. They know what is expected of them and are able to comply. Most students like this life and feel secure within the school.

AS A PARENT
- As your children embark on the middle school years, assure them that everyone who is new to middle school feels frightened
- Let them know teachers and other school staff are there to help
- Discuss extracurricular activities they may like to join
- Get them excited about trying new clubs or social events
- Assure them they will make new friends and have fun in the process
- Expect them to be more independent at home
- Help them organize by making sure they have school supplies
- As a way of staying connected, ask them specific questions about their school day

Note About the Student
Sixth graders often feel overwhelmed by these new freedoms in their lives. Sometimes academic achievement can be affected. Let your children know they

are expected to perform to the best of their abilities. Enforce these rules by taking away privileges if grades begin to slip. Your children should know academic responsibility is their first priority.

It is good to assist your children at home by asking about assignments and checking over homework. It is not advisable to go to classrooms to offer assistance. This only serves to enable and embarrass most students. If you have a concern about your child, email or call the teachers. They will be happy to talk with you about ways to help your child succeed.

> *Parents of sixth graders often have their own anxiety. Most know their children will be expected to perform at a higher level, and want to help children adjust to new responsibilities.*
>
> *Be patient, in time everyone relaxes into these new roles.*

Common Seventh Grade Characteristics

Seventh grade students are the true middle graders. Most have grown out of being amiable teacher and parent pleasers. These students are becoming their own people. They understand the freedoms that middle school offers and feel secure in their place within the school. Seventh grade is a time when students routinely choose different peer groups, different activities, and place new demands on you to allow them to explore.

As their bodies and minds change, their emotions can be extremely intense. These changes can cause them to be impulsive and moody. Boys and girls each experience these behaviors in different ways.

Boys

By now, many boys in this group have learned to disarm you with their charm. If they find themselves in trouble, they will use their history of charming you to gain favor. Keep in mind as charming and sweet as they are, they still must adhere to rules.

Boys of this age group are more likely to become angry over small matters. They often find it difficult to control their emotions and minor situations can become explosive. To avoid more emotional outbursts, it is best not to provoke them. Give them time to regain their composure. If your child has a history of being angry, speak with the school counselor. Most schools offer classes in anger management.

Girls

Seventh grade girls often form strong friendships. They generally want their best friend with them at all times. It can seem trivial to adults, but these friendships are serious to them. Be respectful; acknowledge and include your daughter's friends when possible.

Girls in this group are more likely to grow sad, angry, or emotional for no apparent reason. It most likely has to do with hormone levels. It is best to give them space to play out their feelings. They generally recover in a matter of minutes. Sometimes these feelings persist and need to be addressed. Again, the school counselor can help to get to the root of the problem and find interventions if needed.

AS A PARENT
- Allow your children to explore new things as long as you feel they are safe
- Remember their emotions can be intense; be understanding and respectful
- Give them space to resolve their emotions
- Talk with your children about their feelings
- Get your children help if needed

A Note About the Student
Sometimes new peer groups and activities can interfere with academic achievement. Remind your children that they are expected to maintain their grades. Let them know you are serious by taking away privileges if their grades begin to slip. Make sure your children know academic responsibility is their first priority at school.

Common Eighth Grade Characteristics
Eighth grade is a big year for students. They feel they rule the school and enjoy this new role. Most have a history of established friendships, routines, and a sense of belonging. Eighth graders experience excitement about their "top dog" status and feel confident in this role.

In general, these students have learned to cope with the changes taking place in their bodies and minds. They are more comfortable with themselves as they develop a level of maturity not seen in sixth or seventh graders. They know high school is on the horizon. The anticipation of this move creates a level of energy that builds as the year progresses.

By eighth grade, students are becoming independent thinkers. Most no longer mimic the views of the adults in their lives. Many feel at ease offering their opinions on real issues. They are sensitive to social injustice, and like to discuss global concerns and debate age-old social problems.

Eighth grade is a great time for you as a parent. As your children develop into young adults, you are able to communicate on a new level. Talk with them about their views on current events or discuss matters of concern to society in general. Give them opportunities to express and share their thoughts in a comfortable, safe environment.

These discussions offer insight into your child's personality and views on life. Many parents feel a renewed sense of pride as they catch a glimmer of adult attitudes and thoughts within their child.

AS A PARENT
- Spend quality time with children to strengthen and deepen your relationship
- Volunteer, coach their sports team, or complete a project together
- Discuss age appropriate local and national news events

- Be respectful of their opinions, even if they differ from yours

A Note About the Student

With high school approaching, it is important for children to maintain good study habits. Continue to remind them they are expected to perform to the best of their abilities. Let them know you are serious by taking away privileges if their grades begin to slip. Make sure your children know passing grades are their first priority in school.

A Special Note About Adolescent Life

Every parent wants a happy, well-adjusted child. Concerned parents know adolescence can be a time of uncertainty for some children. A small percentage of adolescents feel isolated from school or home life. It is important for your child to have a sense of belonging. If your child has few or no friends, or appears withdrawn, ask the school counselor to intervene. If school officials are unable to help your child, ask them to recommend resources that can help. Your child's well-being and self-esteem can be heightened through your attentiveness to their issues.

The Impact of Body Changes

Parents, this section was written as a reminder of how awkward it can feel to be an adolescent. As you read through this section, try to recall some of the uncomfortable situations you dealt with during these growing years.

If you think hard enough, it's likely you'll remember girls and boys from this period of your life that were too mature or immature for their age. You may recall the tall boy with clumsy limbs, and perpetual acne or the shy girl whose breasts seemed to develop overnight leaving her feeling self-conscious and vulnerable to suggestive comments of others.

You may remember those rumored to be experimenting with sex, and all the innuendo, gossip and intrigue that went along with this adult topic.

In all sincerity, this chapter will not tell you anything you do not already know. Rather the intent of this section is to help you summon up some of those uncomfortable feelings of the adolescent years. To remind you what it felt like to walk in the shoes of a self-conscious youth and, to lead you to a more personal understanding of your child during this time of intense emotional and physical growth.

Help Your Children Succeed By Understanding

2

THE IMPACT OF BODY CHANGES

The timing of puberty is unique to each child. Some children began to experience body changes in elementary school while others do not have significant changes until they are older.

Puberty brings about many hormonal changes for boys and girls. Their bodies and minds change as they develop into young adults. An increase in hormones can lead to intense feelings and emotional outbursts including anger, sadness, or moodiness. Children generally recover quickly from these outbursts and normally go about their day.

This is also the time when boys and girls become attracted to each other. This attraction creates unfamiliar feelings. For some these feelings lead to uncertainty, shyness, or embarrassment, while others embrace these new feelings and become more extraverted and social.

Girls

In as little as three months a girl's body can develop into a young woman. As the girl gets used to her newly developed shape and body image, she may feel excited about looking more womanly. Some girls feel happy yet self-conscious about their shape. Others enjoy this change and dress to show their shapely bodies.

Some girls do not experience bodily changes until they are older. They may see the developed bodies of friends and have feelings of inadequacy. This delay in maturing can bring about self-esteem and body image issues. If your daughter's body is late to develop, reassure her that she is a lovely young woman and that her body will change in time. Let her know that most development is hereditary. Mothers, share with your daughter the age you were when your body began to mature. Tell her it is likely her body will mature around the same age.

Many young women begin menstruation during young adolescence. Some handle the onset of womanhood without incident while others have premenstrual syndrome (PMS) to the point of tears, emotional outbursts, or anger. Young women are new to these feelings, and it takes time to learn how to manage them. Speak with your daughter about these issues. Let her know she is normal. If her symptoms warrant, seek advice from a pediatrician.

Boys

This is also a time for many changes within a young man's body. In a matter of months, a boy can grow several inches taller. This growth brings longer limbs and stronger bodies. While young men generally enjoy their new body size, it can be an awkward time for them too. Many boys do not know how to manage their longer limbs or new found strength. Sometimes they appear clumsy as their motor skills adjust to the increased size. This lack of coordination can leave them feeling self-conscious and embarrassed.

Some boys do not grow taller until they are much older. They may have tall friends and feel insecure about being shorter. Self-esteem may suffer as they wish to be taller. These boys often act more aggressively than bigger boys, seemingly as a way of proving they are strong and tough. If your son is late to mature, assure him that his body will grow in time. Let him know that most body development is hereditary. Fathers, share with your son the age you were when your body began to mature. Tell him it is likely his body will mature at about the same age.

Hormonal changes are taking place in the male body too. Voices will change and grow into that of young men. Chests will broaden; muscles will strengthen; and, more hair will be visible on the body. Hormones may cause intense feelings of anger to arise and recede quickly. Be understanding, yet firm, as your child learns to manage these emotions.

AS A PARENT

Most adolescents are excited, yet self-conscious about body changes. They embarrass easily and are sensitive to teasing. Parent attitudes and comments strongly influence how children perceive themselves. Positive reinforcement helps build self-esteem and makes children more comfortable with these changes.

Along with being self-conscious or shy about changes in the body, privacy is a big issue among this age group. Most adolescents desire privacy when dressing. Sometimes parents forget their child is growing into a young adult. Many adolescent conversations revolve around parents barging into rooms before knocking. Be supportive and respect your child's privacy when it relates to the body.

Always, reassure your children that they can talk with you. Let them know they are normal in whatever changes are taking place. If your children are too shy or embarrassed to discuss these changes with you, look to your family, school, or church for an adult they trust. It is important that your children have someone to talk with as they grow into adulthood.

There are also many books on puberty in libraries and bookstores you can borrow or purchase. Books are a good way for children to get answers to questions they may be too embarrassed to ask. Be sensitive to their feelings and modesty as they grow to feel comfortable in their new bodies.

As the body develops and romantic feelings emerge, it is a good time to reinforce your family values. Let your children know what is expected from them as they mature. Be sure your children observe you living values consistent with what is expected of them.

Help Your Children Succeed
By Offering

3

A SOLID FOUNDATION

As middle school children deal with exciting and un-predictable changes, they are best equipped to handle these changes when their physical environment is fa-miliar and consistent. They seek comfort in things they can rely on such as knowing friends at school and rou-tines in the home. A solid foundation offers a sense of security and belonging in their outside world, as their inside world is being transformed.

Yet, sometimes major change cannot be avoided. Two common life changes that children face are a move to a new location and a break-up in the family unit. Either of these situations can shake up a child's foundation and sense of security. There are steps a parent can take to help their child deal with unwanted change.

Unavoidable Move

If a family relocation is unavoidable, attempt to cre-ate a sense of control in the situation for your child. One way is to make choosing the new home a decision in which each family member has a say. Selecting the new home as a team will foster a sense of togetherness and connection for the family during this transitional time.

Once your home is chosen, view your child's new school online. Read about the sports teams, extracurricular activities and teachers to get an impression of the school. Get your child excited about trying new activities and meeting new friends by talking about the new school with him or her. At the first opportunity, tour the school campus with your child. When possible, purchase school spirit-wear such as, t-shirts, hats and water bottles to help your child feel part of the school community. Being familiar with the school will ease some of the apprehensions your child has related to change.

Become familiar with the community by driving through the new neighborhood each evening for a few days. Point out locations of interest like the community pool, recreation area or local ice cream shop. Identify the location of the bus stop in relationship to your home. Your child will feel less stress as the neighborhood becomes more recognizable.

Keep in mind, the more control your child has, the better he or she will feel about the change. As the move draws closer, invite your child to be a contributing member of the move by assisting with chores like, packing, labeling and stacking boxes. The more children participate, the more they "buy-in" to the move.

On moving day, your child will be anxious to get his or her room in order. Take time to find boxes of your child's belongings. Offer to help your child unpack as he or she finds places for personal items. Give suggestions on placement of furniture and pictures. The sooner the room is in order, the sooner the child will begin to feel at home.

Change is difficult for everyone no matter the age. Help your child stay connected and involved by recognizing the importance of friendships.

Encourage your child to email or call friends to describe the new home. Help your child feel excited about the change by inviting their friends to come see the new home through play dates or sleepovers. Remember that friendships and social outlets are vital for this age group. Do all you can to keep your child's relationships intact.

Family Break Up

Divorce or a break up can have a major impact on a child's life. Adolescents tend to be sensitive. When a family separation is imminent, many children feel guilty and ask if they are to blame. They wonder what they could have done to prevent the break up. Provide reassurance and let them know they are not responsible.

Some adolescents internalize the situation and will not speak of it. They act as if they are not concerned or worried. Be sure to talk with them. Let your child know your feelings and why you feel this change is best for the family. Ask what you can do to help them. Ask if they want to talk with another family member, a grandparent or older sibling, about their feelings. It is important they have someone to talk with when they are ready.

On the other hand, some children resent and blame one or both parents. These youths want to know why this happened, why it could not be avoided, and who is to blame. They will likely ask both parents the same questions. Be honest. In age appropriate ways, tell them why the break up occurred. Answer their questions and help them understand.

In all situations, be respectful of your child's feelings. Encourage open discussion and be available when your child wants to talk. Listen as your child shares thoughts, feelings and concerns. Give reassurance that both parents will always love him or her.

A few children will display anger over a break-up. It is best not to be drawn into an argument over this topic. Acknowledge and understand their right to be angry. Know that your child is dealing with strong emotions and trying to cope. Respect your child's right to express feelings of anger and sadness.

Refrain from speaking negatively about the other parent. It is not productive or healthy for your child to be used as a messenger between parents. Be a good role model for your child in this situation. Demonstrate integrity and dignity as your family works through this difficult time.

As with any major change, let the school administration, teachers and counselors know the stress your child is under. There may be counseling groups or targeted meetings your child can attend to help work through this confusing time.

Any unwelcome change can upset a child's foundation. Listed are daily routines parents can put into place which offer stability.

Habits That Create a Sense of Stability
- Tell your children you love them daily
- Stay connected by engaging in family events

- Listen when your children want to talk
- Watch for changes in eating or sleeping
- Be consistent in your expectations and discipline
- Create a daily and weekly routine in the home
- Maintain the same connections with social groups, church, ball teams, and clubs
- Encourage your child to spend time with people to whom they feel connected

AS A PARENT

If major change is unavoidable in your family's life, let children know as soon as possible. They need time to adjust to new developments. Talk with children in depth about why change is necessary and how it benefits the family as a whole.

With any transition, ask your children how you can help to make the change less stressful for them. Listen and be sensitive to their concerns. Offer compromise when able. Allow them to take part in decision-making as plans are made. It will help create a sense of inclusion as the family works toward this change together.

Help Your Children Succeed by Recognizing

4

ADOLESCENT SLEEP HABITS

It will come as no surprise to learn that a young adult's sleep habits are counterproductive to student life. Hormonal affects of puberty can cause changes in slumber patterns. These changes often make it difficult to fall asleep at night or wake easily in the morning.

According to the Mayo Clinic, an adolescent's body requires 9 to 10 hours of sleep to feel completely rested. Yet, the majority of students average 2 to 3 hours less rest than needed. This lack of sleep not only hinders mental and physical growth, but also leaves them feeling moody, irritable, and drowsy.

Academic success is affected by sleep patterns too. One important purpose of sleep is to allow the mind to process and understand new concepts. Without the proper amount of rest, the mind cannot readily process new ideas.

Frequent sleep deprivation further impedes learning as students suffer from loss of concentration, poor comprehension, and a lack of attentiveness.

As any parent can tell you, adolescents are often difficult to awaken in the morning. Most need several nudges before they will drag themselves from bed. These students often stumble into school like sleep-walking zombies. Their natural rhythm is to blame as research suggests they aren't fully awake until around 10:00 A.M.

This age group has yet another biological disadvantage that takes place in the evening. Their bodies' natural rhythm causes a surge of energy around 9:00 P.M. During this time when they should be gearing down for rest, their minds are often wide-awake seeking stimulation. This surge of energy can last for two or three hours.

> *Maybe this explains why many of you have found your children playing on the computer, texting, or watching television when you thought they were sleeping.*

With these sleep factors being present, is it any wonder adolescents feel sleep deprived? The good news is there are routines you can put into place which lead to better sleep habits.

Habits that Can Aid Sleep
- Set a standard bedtime
- Gear down 30-45 minutes before bedtime
- Stay close to the regular bedtime schedule on weekends
- Turn off TV, phone, and computer
- Read or listen to soothing music

- A small glass of warm milks acts as a sedative for some children
- A warm shower before bed helps to aid in relaxation
- Make sure the bed is comfortable
- Sleep in a dark room
- Discourage naps during the day
- Set a consistent wake-up time
- Be a good role model by adhering to a regular bedtime yourself

AS A PARENT

In the human body, brain cells work together to create the biological clock. The natural rhythm of this clock can be manipulated to a small degree by exposure to darkness and light. It is important for your children to set their body's natural clock by waking at the same time each morning. This consistency will help create regular sleep habits.

Upon waking each morning, turn on bright lights or open windows as a way of letting the body know it is time to rise. Offer your child something cool to drink to assist the body system in waking. Get your child talking as a way of clearing the haze and allowing the brain to be awake for learning.

Help Your Children Succeed by Recognizing The Need For

5

ORGANIZATION

At this age, even the best of students can be disorganized. They have several academic classes, different classrooms, teachers, books, and materials. For the first time, the students have independence to move freely through the halls and common areas. Even those who were fairly organized in elementary school can find themselves overwhelmed. In middle schools, missing items are commonplace. The lost and found bins topple over with sweaters, jackets, and notebooks.

Organization is part of the education process and is directly related to academic success. One of the easiest fixes that affect grades is turning assignments in on time. Many times students do class and homework assignments, but fail to turn in the work. There are a variety of excuses teachers hear for missing work such as, it was left at home, it was lost in their locker, the work was left at a friend's house, or sometimes students simply have no idea where they left the work.

When missing assignments are not found or redone, teachers have no choice but to put a zero in the grade book. Parents, you can do the math and see that even the grades of good students are affected by missed work. It is extremely important that students be organized in order to get assignments done properly and turned in on time.

Ways to Help Your Child Organize

In the Home:
- Create a place for papers that are brought home from school
- Designate an area for your child to do homework
- Have a specific place for items that need to be signed and returned to school
- Ask your child to clean out book bags, and notebooks *weekly*
- Make sure completed homework goes into book bags

In School:
- Have your child write assignments in a notebook or agenda
- Purchase different color folders for each class in your child's schedule
- Ask your child to check the lost and found bins as soon as he/she notices items are missing

Before Bedtime:
Pack book bags with items needed for school
Have children shower or bathe in the evening
Lay out clothes needed for the morning

AS A PARENT

Be respectful. Refrain from labeling your children as hopeless or forgetful. This only serves to belittle them. Offer structure by having routine in the home. Expect your children to be responsible for specific chores. Be specific on how you want chores accomplished. Ask your children to repeat directions back to you before they begin. Instead of saying, "Clean the kitchen", you might say, "Wash the dishes, and leave them to dry," or "Wash and dry the dishes before putting them away." Structure allows children to think more clearly and, in turn, learn to be more organized.

> When the class dismissal bell rings, teachers raise their voice over the din of movement reminding students to take all personal items. As the class rushes to beat the tardy bell, inevitable items are left behind. *Such is life in middle school*

The nature of this age group lends itself to disorganization. Your children may likely be doing the best they can on a given day. Work with them and over time they will learn skills to be more responsible.

Help Your Children Succeed by Understanding

6

IMPULSIVE BEHAVIORS

Middle school boys and girls often make impulsive decisions without considering the consequences. Most times these acts are harmless; occasionally they are dangerous or destructive. Children show remorse when caught, but generally can offer no reason for their poor judgment. Authority figures are often upset and frustrated by these acts. In reality, impulsive behavior is a normal part of puberty.

Many people naturally assume that adolescents are simply small versions of adults. This assumption is false. Like the body, the brain must mature into adulthood. The part of the brain responsible for decision-making is still developing during adolescence. Therefore, young people often act from emotion rather than reason.

Examples of Impulsive Behavior May Include
- Going home with a friend without permission
- Walking home from school without asking
- Getting into a fight over a minor issue
- Skipping classes or school
- Getting angry over something minor

- Lashing out at an authority figure
- Crying over something trivial (Yes, boys too)

> *Experts in child development agree that more risky impulsive behaviors are likely to occur when adolescents are among peers, and away from adult eyes. Without supervision, children are as much as twice as likely to engage in unsafe behaviors. While children desire and need a level of independence, parents should be aware of children's whereabouts and activities at all times.*

AS A PARENT

In truth, children may act impulsively in a number of ways. If your children act without thinking or make poor choices, remember it is a normal part of adolescence. Be understanding, but continue to offer consequences for poor behavior. Remind them to take time to *think* before they act.

Reinforce what is expected by reviewing your family rules and values often. Let children know these rules are for their safety and well-being. Be firm with your discipline, yet patient with your understanding. Over time, your children will grow to make more reasonable choices.

Help Your Children Succeed by Following Through With

7

DISCIPLINE

Solid discipline allows parents to reward good behaviors and set consequences for poor ones. Parental supervision and follow-through are essential for children to learn appropriate conduct. When parents expect and model good behavior, they find their children's behavior improves. It is important to be fair, consistent, and loving in your efforts. Your children's safety and happiness depend on your ability to teach them to act responsibly.

Discipline can be tricky with middle school children. Impulsive behaviors and under-developed decision making skills can lead to poor choices. Once in hot water, this age group will go to great lengths to avoid punishment. Repeat offenders learn to think quickly and talk fast as a means of diversion. They are known to cry, blame, or lie in an attempt to escape trouble. If all else fails, they will try to negotiate the consequences.

As the parent, maintain control of any discussion concerning your children's poor behavior. Listen attentively to their side of the story. Ask appropriate questions and call other children or parents if needed to get a true perspective. When it is time to discipline your children leave no room for discussion, be authoritative, firm and consistent with consequences.

The way you respond when angry serves as a model for your children. It demonstrates the way you want them to handle themselves. If you find you are too angry to talk, ask your child to leave the room as you take the time to calm down. It is advisable to refrain from setting consequences until you are in control of your emotions.

There is not a situation where verbal abuse or physical contact is appropriate. A parent's out of control behavior does not help resolve issues; it only serves as poor modeling for children. They will turn this form of anger on you and others in the future. If your children's temper gets out of control, calmly tell them you will talk when they calm down. Ask them to leave the room and return when they can talk sensibly. Remember, you are the adult. Maintain control of any disagreements and keep your voice even and authoritative as you speak with your children.

Discipline Suggestions
- Remove electronics; phones, computers, TV, and MP3 players
- Take away privileges to outings or events
- Allow no visits or calls from friend
- Restrict them from participating in after school or weekend recreational activities
- Increase the chores at home to help build Responsibility

- If the poor behavior warrants, have the child write a short essay or research paper about the offence that occurred and how it should have been handled differently

Note to Parent

Sometimes parents forget their children are older and may choose punishments more suited for younger children. It is generally not advisable to have middle school children go to their rooms for punishment. Most adolescents prefer to be in their rooms, so you are actually rewarding and reinforcing their poor behavior. A better choice would be to have them spend more time helping with chores or projects around the house.

Remain firm, fair, loving, and consistent in your discipline decisions. Your follow-through now will make the teen years ahead more enjoyable and serve to raise a happier more responsible adult.

Two Points of a Serious Nature

To this point, this handbook has shared some of the more common challenges that middle school students and their parents face. There are two issues of a serious nature that need to be addressed. These are real concerns that teachers face each year. These issues only apply to a small portion of the population, but if your children fall into this group, it is in their best interest that you are informed.

These concerns have the potential to change the course of a child's life.

Help Your Children Succeed by Monitoring

8

ACADEMIC GRADES

First is the issue of failing academic classes. Each semester a child's poor grades are allowed to go unaddressed, the child falls further and further behind. Over time, it becomes more difficult for the student to recover. Chronic failing grades are detrimental to academic success, self-esteem, and social acceptance.

The sad truth is, if children exit eighth grade with a pattern of failing classes, low attendance, apathy or poor self-esteem, *it is extremely likely they will drop out of high school.* High school demands a higher level of responsibility including strong study skills and self-discipline. Students who fail to develop these skills in middle school will find it difficult to cope in the high school setting.

Failing Students Exhibit One of Three Behaviors in Class

- The child will quietly sit at his or her desk in an attempt to be invisible to the teacher and other students. As this pattern continues day after day, the student will become more withdrawn.

- A student sometimes acts as class clown in an attempt to take the attention off the fact he or she has nothing to offer in class. This serves to make others laugh, but also keeps the student behind in class work.
- The student may choose to be disruptive. He or she may talk out of turn, whisper to classmates, walk around the room, or repeatedly ask off-subject questions as a means of avoiding work.

In these situations, teachers do what they can to help students to be successful. Teachers may involve students in small group activities, pair them with a peer tutor, give them special assignments or offer personal tutoring.

A student who exhibits failing behaviors in one class generally repeats these behaviors in other classes. If this pattern continues with no intervention, he or she will eventually be held back. Retention is detrimental for students both emotionally and academically. It results in the loss of grade level peers and a sense of belonging. Peers move forward while the failing student's life goes into repeat mode. The child feels embarrassed, hopeless, and ultimately abandoned.

These feelings of inadequacy can lead students to seek peer groups in which academic success is not valued. These groups are often involved in destructive activities such as gangs, drugs, sex, or petty crime.

For students with a pattern of poor grades, there are school programs in place that offer assistance. Some schools offer morning, afternoon, or mid-day tutoring. There are also counselors and academic coaches who can intervene to help your children find the resources they need. Talk with your children's teachers or counselors to take advantage of these resources. It is imperative to your children's future that you reach out to the school for help.

Communicate with teachers daily to get your children's class and homework assignments. Email allows direct communication; hence, it is the best method. However, correspondence through notes or phone calls also work well. Teachers will be more than willing to help. Like you, they want what's best for your children.

If your children have a history of low or failing grades, they will adamantly resist your interest in their education. Be firm in your decision to help them get on track. Your support is needed for them to be successful. They most likely have a poor work ethic and inadequate study skills. It is essential that you provide clear expectations and consistent discipline where grades are concerned.

Steps to Help Your Child Succeed

- Set academic expectations; take away privileges when expectations are not met
- To be successful, your children must be present in school; be persistent and require your children to attend class each day
- Require them to take advantage of academic resources at school; follow though to be sure they participate
- Have a set homework time; review your children's completed homework

- Ask the teacher what topics are being studied in class; discuss these topics with your children
- Whenever possible, volunteer at your children's school library or front office, your presence in the building shows your commitment to their success
- Offer rewards for improved performance; celebrate all achievements no matter how small

Remain strong and authoritative with your children. They cannot succeed without your guidance and steadfast support.

Those with a history of failing grades generally have hopeless attitudes. They need your unwavering assurance that they can succeed. Let them know that while excellent grades are optimal, improved grades are acceptable. Remember to praise and recognize large and small successes. As grades continue to improve, your children will grow more confident and proud of their accomplishments.

Help Your Children Succeed By Addressing

9

POOR CHOICES

The second concern teachers face is watching students make poor choices. Teachers see your children daily. They observe your children's interactions with others in a variety of settings, social, academic, structured, and unstructured. Based on these interactions, teachers have a good idea of your child's nature and personality.

Many times, teachers are the first adults to observe when a student exhibits uncharacteristic behaviors. A child that was once friendly may become withdrawn, choose a new peer group, or become less concerned with grades. Any of these can be signs that something is different in a child's life.

If the situation persists over a few days, most teachers will call the parent to share their concerns and ask the school counselor to intervene. School counselors are good at getting to the heart of matters. Many times a middle school student's unusual behavior is due to hormonal changes that cause minor things to get blown out of portion. He or she may be upset over friendships, issues at home, or a low grade in school.

In a small number of cases these behaviors indicate something more serious like drug use, sexual misconduct, or gang initiation. If one of these situations is present, it is critical the child gets assistance. The schools have resources that can help. Early intervention is the best way to protect a child's future.

Be engaged in your children's lives. It is the best way to keep them safe. Make a habit of spending quality time together. Create the type of home environment where your children's friends want to spend their time too.

Ways to Stay Engaged
- Schedule regular family activities where your children are expected to participate
- Get them involved in team sports and attend the games
- Coach their sports team
- Create a weekly family appreciation day to play games, go to the library, or see a movie
- Find local activities or hobbies that you can enjoy together
- Recognize and support their relationships with friends of whom you approve
- Get to know the parents of your children's friends
- Ask children open ended questions as a means of better communication

AS A PARENT

Let your children know they are important. A good time to bond is at dinner or before bed. Take the lead and talk with them about your work, childhood memories, or upcoming events. Even if they seem uninterested, do not be deterred. In time, most children will recognize this interaction as a daily routine and begin to open up.

10

Conclusion

The adolescent years are the last years of childhood. Embrace and enjoy this time in your children's lives. Remember to be firm and consistent in discipline. Teach them boundaries to keep them safe. Some of the behaviors that anger you now will develop into stories your family laughs about in the future.

Aid in your children's transition into adulthood. Support their social nature, by getting them engaged in activities that interest them. These activities create a safe, controlled environment where they can grow and learn.

If finances are an issue, most schools offer activities or clubs at no cost. Additionally, many sports and music programs offer scholarships. Ask school staff, the neighborhood Y.M.C.A., or local Girls and Boys Clubs for assistance. These organizations will be able to offer suggestions on available resources.

In closing, the middle school years are an important time in a child's life. This phase of life is both rewarding and challenging. As adolescents grow from children to young adults, their personalities begin to emerge. They discover their sense of belonging and begin to grow more secure with themselves. It is up to the adults in their lives to create a healthy balance of staying close emotionally while giving children room to develop. These young adults need to be offered love, understanding, and support every step of the way. Sometimes just knowing someone cares is all a child needs to thrive.

"Parenting is the cornerstone for shaping the life of a child. How we shape that life is how we shape the world."

Becky Kapsalis

Resources:

Chapter 2
Puberty: Whole Lotta Changin' Goin' On PBS Kids, It's My Life. Accessed July 2009.

Chapter 4
Teen Sleep: Why is your teen so tired? Mayo Clinic. Accessed July 2009. (Staff Writer)

Chapter 6
Adolescent Brain Development: The Importance of Parental Involvement: prepared by John Snow Inc. Accessed July 2009.

Chapter 8
Putting Middle Grades Students on the Graduation Path, A Policy and Practice Brief, Robert Balfanz, Everyone Graduates Center Accessed July 2009.

For more in depth information on topics covered in the handbook view the sites listed below.

The Mayo Clinic offers information and tips on sleep habits of youth.
http://www.mayoclinic.com/

PBS Kids is a great resource for information on and for adolescents.
http://pbskids.org/itsmylife/body/puberty/index.html

John Snow Inc. offers great information on brain development.
http://www.hhs.gov/opa/familylife/annualconfab stracts/brain_dvt_white_paper.pdf

Robert Balfanz of John Hopkins University put together an eye opening study on academics and the middle school years.
http://www.nmsa.org/portals/0/pdf/research/ Research_from_the_Field/Policy_Brief_Balfanz.pdf

Resources for Parents:

http://www.parenting.org/

http://www.psparents.net/middle school.htm

http://www.tweenparent.com/

http://parentteacherpartnerships.blogspot.com/

http://www.education.com/

Resources for Teachers:

http://www.edarticle.com/

http://www.naeducation.org/

http://www.ed.gov/

http://www.examiner.com/x-11234-Public-Education-Examiner?showbio

http://www.nasa.gov/offices/education/about/index.html

Recommended Reading for Parents:

Child and Adolescent Development: An Advanced Course by William Damon and Richard M. Lerner

The Adolescent: Development, Relationships, and Culture (13th Edition) (My Development Lab Series) by Kim Gale Dolgin

Child and Adolescent Development: A Chronological Approach by Danuta Bukatko (**Hardcover** – Jan. 2, 2007)

Handbook of Adolescent Psychology, Individual Bases of Adolescent Development (Volume 1) by Richard M. Lerner and Laurence Steinberg (**Hardcover** – Apr. 6, 2009)

These two books offer a more humorous version on Adolescence:

How to Hug a Porcupine: Negotiating the Prickly Points of the Tween Years by Julie A. Ross

The Everything Tween Book: A Parent's Guide to Surviving the Turbulent Pre-Teen Years (Everything Series) by Linda Sonna

Recommended Reading For The Middle School Student:

The Middle School Survival Guide: How to Survive from the Day Elementary School Ends until the Second High School Begins by Arlene Erlbach and Helen Flook (**Paperback** – Aug. 1, 2003)

Worst-Case Scenario Survival Handbook, The: Middle School (Worst Case Scenario Junior Editions) by Robin Epstein and Ben H. Winters (**Paperback** – June 17, 2009)

Too Old for This, Too Young for That! Your Survival Guide for the Middle-School Years by Harriet S. Mosatche and Karen Unger

The Middle School Student's Guide to Ruling the World! By Susan Mulcaire

Acknowledgements

I would like to offer a special thanks to those who offered their expertise and advice in the development of this handbook.

Dr. Peggy Norman, Director Education division Cairo University.

Tracy Horton, Ed.S, Middle school Counselor, Catoosa County, Georgia.

Ismahen Kangles, M.Ed. Director of Middle School for a New Society, the Public Education foundation, Hamilton County Schools, Tennessee.

Dr. Jeffrey A Betman PhD., child psychologist, Farmington Hills Michigan.

Dr. Nancy Johnson MD, pediatrics, Gainesville, Georgia.

Resources

Your school system, community school, home school organization, PTA, parenting group or non-profit can receive copies of this book for training or giveaway at special discounted pricing, great service and direct shipping.

Get information about discounted bulk sales of this handbook at
www.thrivingstudent.com.

Victoria Cummings M.Ed

Victoria earned her under graduate and graduate degrees in education from Mercer University in Atlanta, Georgia. She became an educator in 1988, and quickly began to excel in her career. In this role she taught students in all grade levels from primary to middle school. These classroom positions evolved into leadership roles where she lead parent and teacher workshops, and later became director of school based programs.

After spending more than twenty years in the education system, Victoria is now a parenting coach whose focus is on academic success. Through individual and group coaching she listens to parent concerns and offers insights, advice and strategies on how to foster happier more academically successful children.

Victoria has written this handbook for parents of the often-misunderstood middle school learner in an effort to help parents successfully navigate their adolescent through these challenging years.

Contact Victoria at
victoria@thrivingstudent.com